# Russian Tortoise

# Books by Gardner McFall

**Poetry**
The Pilot's Daughter   (1996)
Russian Tortoise   (2009)

**Children's Books**
Jonathan's Cloud   (1986)
Naming the Animals   (1994)

**Criticism**
Made with Words, by May Swenson, Editor   (1998)
The Wind in the Willows, by Kenneth Grahame, Introduction and Notes   (2005)

# Russian Tortoise

**Gardner McFall**

# TIME BEING BOOKS
**POETRY IN SIGHT AND SOUND**

*An imprint of Time Being Press*
St. Louis, Missouri

Copyright © 2009 by Gardner McFall

All rights reserved under International and Pan-American Copyright Conventions. No part of this book shall be reproduced in any form (except by reviewers for the public press) without written permission from the publisher:

       Time Being Books®
       10411 Clayton Road
       St. Louis, Missouri 63131

Time Being Books® is an imprint of Time Being Press®, St. Louis, Missouri.

Time Being Press® is a 501(c)(3) not-for-profit corporation.

Time Being Books® volumes are printed on acid-free paper.

ISBN 978-1-56809-119-8 (paperback)

Library of Congress Cataloging-in-Publication Data:
McFall, Gardner.
    Russian tortoise / Gardner McFall. — 1st ed.
       p. cm.
    ISBN: 978-1-56809-119-8 (alk. paper)
    I. Title.
    PS3563.C3624R87 2009
    811'.54—dc22
                                                    2009005246

Cover design by Claudia Carlson. www.claudiagraphics.com
Cover sketch by William Berryman, "View of River with Bridge," c. 1812,
   courtesy of the Library of Congress, LC-USZC4-4983
Author photo by Susan Unterberg
Book design and typesetting by Trilogy M. Mattson

Manufactured in the United States of America

First Edition, first printing (2009)

# Acknowledgments

I gratefully acknowledge the publications in which the following poems first appeared: *The Atlantic Monthly* ("Love Work"); *Big City Lit* ("Like a Mantle, the Sea" and "Night Birding, Trinidad"); *Contemporary Poetry of New England* ("Album" and "In Mountain Air"); *Hanging Loose* ("Russian Tortoise"); *The New Criterion* ("The Body's Colloquy," "Seaweed Weather (1)" and "Sweet Cure"); *The New York Times* ("Plaza View"); *The Partisan Review* ("The Harvesters"); *Pequod* ("Her Hands," "The Leap" and "Lesson"); *Ploughshares* ("The Scan"); *Poet Lore* ("The Alleluia Man," "Amulet Market," "Begin," "Crossing," "Glistening," "Last Entry," "My Father Meets Amelia Earhart" and "Stopping at the True, the Good, the Beautiful Company in Bac Ninh"); *Poetry NZ* ("Flash"); *Rattapallax* ("Activity That Defies Loss" and "Story of Us"); *River Styx* ("Water Buffalo"); *The Sewanee Review* ("Plates from Audubon's Double Elephant Folio"); *Southwest Review* ("The News"); *Tin House* ("Desire," "First Kiss" and "Weatherworn").

"Seaweed Weather (1)" was reprinted in *Contemporary Poetry of New England*, edited by Robert Pack and Jay Parini, and also in *"For New Orleans" & Other Poems*, edited by Ashis Gupta. "Love Work" was reprinted in *Poetry Calendar 2007*, "Story of Us" in *The Alhambra Poetry Calendar 2008* and "The News" in *The Alhambra Poetry Calendar 2009*, edited by Shafiq Naz. "The News" also appeared in *Poetry Daily*. "Weatherworn" was reprinted in *Satellite Convulsions: Poems from Tin House*, edited by Brenda Shaughnessy and CJ Evans.

I wish to thank the Corporation of Yaddo, for the room and quiet in which to work, and those friends whose generosity and insights lent me renewed energy in completing the manuscript. My thanks, also, to Susan Unterberg, for photographing the tortoise print used in the book's cover design, and to the editors at Time Being Books.

*For my husband,*

*Peter Olberg*

# Contents

## I: Her Hands

Begin   *17*
Her Hands   *18*
Sweet Cure   *20*
My Blue Kerman   *21*
Album   *23*
Crossing   *24*
Like a Mantle, the Sea   *25*
Glistening   *26*


## II. Russian Tortoise

Russian Tortoise   *29*
The Body's Colloquy   *32*
Plates from Audubon's Double Elephant Folio   *33*
Night Birding, Trinidad   *36*
The Scan   *37*
The News   *38*
The Harvesters   *39*
Activity That Defies Loss   *40*
Cleo   *42*
The Leap   *43*
Sign   *45*
Flash   *47*
Amulet Market   *48*
The Alleluia Man   *49*
Last Entry   *51*


## III. War Remnants

Two Halves   *55*
Stopping at the True, the Good, the Beautiful Company in Bac Ninh   *56*

My Father Meets Amelia Earhart    57
Water Buffalo    59
At the War Remnants Museum, Saigon    60
Little Exchange    62
The Moving Wall    63
Eye Exam    65

## IV: Love Work

First Kiss    69
Desire    70
Weatherworn    71
In Mountain Air    72
Seaweed Weather    73
Story of Us    75
Lesson    76
Plaza View    77
Love Work    78

# Russian Tortoise

# I. Her Hands

*To the memory of my mother,
Joan Livingston McFall
(1928-2000)*

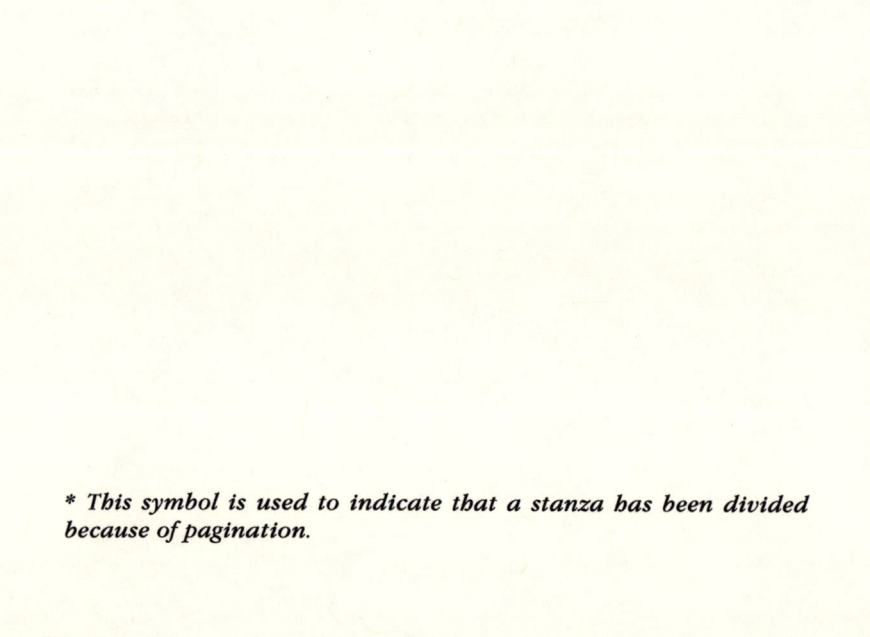

\* *This symbol is used to indicate that a stanza has been divided because of pagination.*

## Begin

A brown bird outside my window
has sung the same tune all morning.
He thinks, like someone speaking English
in a foreign country, if he sings louder
I will understand. He darts from roof

to sill. Does he flick a wing or tip
his head to underscore the meaning?
His five notes — three ascending,
two down, at least, demand: rise,
come to the window. Yet when I do,

he flings himself into a nearby fir.
Left on my own, the sight is what
I expected: terrace, emerald lawn,
and, hard to bear, the marble fountain
where I sat in moonlight, empty,

the girl I once was gone. He's back,
in consort with a friend, asking,
what difference does it really make?
The trees are immense, the sky blue.
The fountain will fill. His five notes:

Haven't you grasped anything yet?
Your life is halfway up; open
the latticework; let all the air in
now, the air that's new and stings
with memory. Trust yourself; begin.

## Her Hands

Her hands, each finger a taper of light, holding
a mesh canvas, weaving her needle's yarn
in and out, coaxing a brave design
where there was none before,
or her hands rolling, kneading the dough, applying
the tin biscuit cutter from her mother's kitchen,
or holding a book, having pushed her glasses like a headband
onto her jet-colored hair, reaching for her tumbler
of water, which she carried everywhere, even in the car
driving; her hands adjusting the mirror, placing
a lit cigarette in the pullout ashtray;
her fluttering hands, perfectly manicured;
later, her hands reaching for a shark's tooth
on the white stretch of beach, her hands on the rim
of her hat to keep it from blowing off as she floated
on the slowly deflating raft, her hands tying
my swimsuit, rubbing Coppertone on my brother's back;
her hands in soapy water, polishing
candlesticks, snapping beans, patting
the soil down in a potted spider plant,
pruning roses, hanging a wreath on our door;
her hands with shining rings, holding a hairbrush,
brushing, buttoning a peignoir, ironing once
a long time ago Father's khaki uniform,
waving good-bye at the hangar with one hand,
the other resting on my shoulder, that night dabbing
her eyes with a handkerchief in front of Ed Sullivan:
the Beatles singing "I Want to Hold Your Hand";
her hands switching off the TV, folding us into bed;
her hands, alone, by themselves, certain;
noting a small appointment in her calendar,
wrapping presents, stacking towels, writing thank-yous,
opening a hymnal, handing me the car keys
and her diamond watch, smoothing my bridal veil;
her hands like tissue paper, with their visible
inland waterway of veins; later,
bruised black and violet at the slightest knock,
patched with Band-Aids; her hands on the mobile IV,
closing her hospital gown in the back, one hand
*

## I: HER HANDS

on the bed to brace herself; her hands resting,
holding her baby pillow to her chest,
plied with needles under the skin and tape,
trailing tubes; her hands suddenly still,
cool to the touch, her hand in my hand,
long, limp as a parched morning star;
a slight pressure, then nothing; her hands growing
dark with blood, with no turning back, her hands
reposed on her heart as though taking a nap.

## Sweet Cure

A man, with a dozen small pieces of paper
compared to my two, knew I was waiting
behind him at the pharmacy xerox machine,
and might have said, "You have so few?
Please go ahead," but feigned ignorance.

I sighed, settling in hot-black impatience,
though he was under duress, documenting his health
for some insurance company bureaucrat.
I observed the back of his crimped neck —
its old man and the sea look, balding head

soft as a baby's, slumped shoulders,
trousers pulled up high with a tightened belt.
His hands unfurled the machine cover
again and again, placing each scrap square
in the center like a photo inside its frame.

I could have advised: fit two on a legal-size page.
Instead, I glanced over the store shelves,
lingered at the Q-tips and lotions,
the bright, flamingo children's aspirin of my youth.
I didn't know they were still being made.

I could see my mother's hand, popping the cap,
dropping two in my palm, taste their sweet,
tangy flight down my throat. How I slipped into bed,
fever lightened by Mother's caress. She sat
until I slept; she must have had work to do, though

what, I'll never know. The man in front of me
gathered his papers and turned to leave
without acknowledging my presence in any way
just as I must have turned from my mother
to the wall and fallen into night's dreams.

## My Blue Kerman

I sprawled on it
as a child, lost
in its arabesques,
the overall design

impossible to discern,
taking it for ground
my stuffed bears loped
across or lolled on.

The rug heard news
of marriages and birth,
who was ill or well;
it muffled angry words,

absorbed Mother's only
piano tune late at night:
"Smoke Gets in Your Eyes."
It warmed three houses,

Grandmother's for which
she bought the rug in 1945,
the cost quite dear,
but dearer the blue Kerman.

She died and it lay
in her curtained living
room, then an extension
of Mother's house, built

to avert the nursing home.
Moved from her three-decade
colonial to a condo half
the size, Mother unfurled it

in her upstairs bedroom
where it spent the last four years,
companionable as a dog,
attuned to her phone calls,

her curses and prayers.
It missed nothing,
not bath water being drawn,
the downstairs doorbell,

or jays outside her window
fronting the solid live oak.
Younger, I coveted the rug,
mindless how ownership

would mean those I loved
were gone. And now it's here,
shipped by UPS, restored
for more than its original

price. Who would know?
It's folded, wrapped, standing
on end in my kitchen corner
like a bandaged, throbbing thumb.

My apartment has no room
that's big enough to hold
this rug when opened up —
indigo blue, still, and rose.

## **Album**

Bring back the long summer after fourth grade
with stinging-cold waves that crashed on the Cape,
the tall, white dunes we scrambled across, the wild
blackberries we picked, a pair of tame pintos
fed clutches of grass over the farmer's gate,
*Little House on the Prairie* devoured in bed —

back the rust-red, overturned rowboat my father
perched upon, wearing Bermuda shorts and a grin
beside my gleaming, willow-thin mother,
tow-headed brother, and me who smiled with ease
at the shutter's click, the future assuredly bright,
back the damp days and salt-air night on the skin
when fog drifted down like a cotton coverlet
and at dawn was gently gathered up again.

## Crossing

After the vessels broke in my mother's brain, flooding
her body like a low-lying delta, what did the angel
pledge? A trade of days for suffering's end,
two children and their own for a mate, parents, friends?
Did sparks or bells erupt in a vision eluding us?
Her agonal breath rose and fell in a final rhapsody,
drowning every other sound and sight. At her bed
we whispered, *do what you must; we'll be fine.*

Little wings in a box — open it, they fly
like the spirit out of the body. Red light on the tracks
of the crossing. She's gone. She's not coming back.
Conductor, if you have ears or eyes, you do not need
my telling whom you have taken, what care must be given,
since you have carried her off without any books,
crosswords, or the leaping white dog she loved to walk.

## Like a Mantle, the Sea

Between the parentheses of birth and perishing
I am halfway, in a sentence whose meaning escapes,
nature's pattern not indiscernible, but hard
to accept, at least on this morning, when I feel
unprepared to greet the other side of what little
time and space I occupy. True, I have already
met what I thought myself unequal to:
a father's disappearance, the birth of a child,
a mother's death. How can *she* not be here?
I often think, walking along, wishing to telephone,
her number long since disconnected. How am I
the mother now? I wear the robes loosely.
I am like one of those figures in the narrow boat
in *The Great Wave off Kanagawa* by Hokusai, only
I don't know if they bow in heart-chilling fear as the breaker
curves like a funeral awning over their slender backs
or in mild assent, there between water and water,
skimming the earth, like a mantle, the sea.

## Glistening

Grief is heavy ore,
and what to make of it
requires a miner's skill,

tools for splitting in half,
strength to chip away
rock that hides a gem.

At camp years ago,
I panned for rubies
in a Carolina mine —

rubies, my birthstone —
and found a garnet:
what became of it?

Or the twined gold ring
I made for Mother
in arts & crafts, which she

wore as only a mother
will — I hear her Southern
accent, audible to the heart

that breaks but is well made
by the furnace and weight
of earth, a kind of glistening:

"You are lucky.
I love you.
I am not afraid to die."

## II. Russian Tortoise

## Russian Tortoise

The science teacher's elation at my consenting
to lodge the Russian tortoise for Christmas break
doesn't allay my fears. The prospect ignites
the memory of a friend's well-meaning act
when she gave my dime-store turtles a midday sunbath
and they broiled to death. Hearing this, my child
asserts with the faith of a bird singing in winter
that, unlike my friend, she knows the proper care
of a tortoise. Every day it must be fed
some lettuce and given a bath in a plastic tub.
It needs the heater left on beneath its cage —
just this (what could be simpler?) for the rest
of its life, without variation, which may be why
as we left school, a passing acquaintance said,
Good luck having any rapport with a tortoise.

Observation, the acolyte of affection,
yokes disparate creatures — or so I think, watching
the graceless being that braves whatever comes
his way with determination. For instance, my hand,
divine intervention, which moves him closer
to his food, presents a challenge he takes in stride,
reversing himself on the woodchips toward the log
for a nap, one ungainly step at a time.
His paltry headway suggests he's caught
in an undertow. Only by traveling sideways,
parallel to shore, will he reach his goal.
It's counterintuitive, but true. So his vain
efforts to burrow beneath the log nevertheless
convince him he's quite safely camouflaged
like the foolish people in Eden hiding from God.

Science claims he can live a hundred years,
which means he'll be here after I'm gone and outlive
my daughter, too, assuming he doesn't fall
over the log on his back (a situation
he can't endure long), the heater stays on,
and the custodians, charged with his care, care for him.
These variables beyond his control of which
\*

he is mindless grieve me, resembling as they do
some recipe for a pointless world, where choice
is pared to log or bowl, freedom's exercise
too slight to mention. If only he could count
woodchips, he might be spared relentless boredom
or I could recite the fable in which he stars:
Slow and steady wins the race! He blinks
absently. What is the race he should want to win?

Poor tortoise! Never to have a mate, lay eggs,
or crawl on fear of your life across a road
toward a desirable sip of pond. Never to taste
wild mushrooms or feel pine needles under your nails,
stretch your accordion neck its full length to peer
at moonlight on a forest path, or, hearing
the sound of feet, withdraw — instead to live decades
in this reptilian limbo. I should free you,
release you deep in the park. I could plant you
under a tree, but lacking the kisses and hugs
of schoolgirls, customary waves of attention
and disregard, you'd probably sit, more doorstop
than tortoise, confused by the actual ground and rain.
Parakeets, parrots, Easter rabbits, and snakes,
released by their owners, would congregate as you

recollected your previous life, with all
a storybook's perfection, glossed over
and embellished for effect. Captivity-raised,
you'd soon regret the fresh lettuce, long for
your bathwater, tepid and low, from which
though you paddled the basin's sides, you couldn't climb
without assistance. You'd miss the familiar log.
Sad tortoise, or sad to me, not even once
would you call the air free or make your way downhill
to inspect the reservoir, where children sail boats,
migrating ducks alight, and another tortoise
might be languishing on a sun-drenched bank,
a kindred soul with whom you could relate
or share some authentic tortoise experience we
who study you know nothing about or will know.

## II. RUSSIAN TORTOISE

How hard the task of accepting oneself alone,
one's condition. You've mastered this feat, I guess.
Divested of any illusions, you know what is
reasonable to expect. Since you expect
nothing, you harbor no disappointment,
but live each moment in the glass world you're given —
without shame or remorse, true to your nature,
assenting, and with a degree of clear purpose
that allows you to lift your tiny, olive head
at the sound of my hand opening the top of your cage.
Whenever I place a bright new leaf in your dish,
whether Bibb, Boston, or escarole, you begin
to browse with gusto, making me admire
your automatic jaw, your gray tongue that tastes
self-knowledge. I've come to find you the perfect guest.

## The Body's Colloquy

Inspiration to Mind

Small bird, flying each day to the well
in search of water within your reach,
one dawn, the bucket will be hauled full

so you can bathe and drink your fill,
unsure on what disposition the gift
depends, but sustained by it still.


Mind to Heart

Try to possess just one clear feeling,
not a clot — a single stream or shoot
of falling, mountain water, which pools

silt-settled in a deep-green spot,
apart, shot through with sunlight to
the bottom, where fish wreathe the rock.


Eye to Hand

Regarding beauty, the world will not recite
or recollect my gaze transfixed upon
the full moon rising out of a phosphorous sea,

the coliseum, pyramids, or shrine at Delphi,
my lover's look, my child's wonder at the sun;
servant of sight, take up your pen and write!

## Plates from Audubon's Double Elephant Folio

**1**

Out of the sky like a bolt from an angry god,
a red-shouldered hawk seizes a branch
and turns to eye his mate on the fork above,
concluding an urgent, brief conspiracy.
Audubon captured the swiveled head, the texture
of tufted crown against the grain of his neck,
four expansive talons on each yellow foot,
each talon pointed and black as a fishing hook;
around them: perfectly indifferent leaves
and hanging moss braceleting a limb.
The idea, not merely the shape, he thought,
painting a striking gold around the nostril
high on each bird's rapier mandible —
beneath them, perhaps, a salt-water marsh hen.

**2**

Here, a common buzzard descends on a hare
startled to find the beak an inch away
from his silky head and flushed with only one
impulse: escape; yet as he pivots to stare
the bird in the face, the bank he's crouching on
crumbles into the sluggish river nearby,
across which stands a pale blue house in haze,
timber, cut and stacked — a logger's cabin?
The backdrop looks forever at a remove
from the immediate subject of *sauve qui peut*,
Audubon's theme, concomitant life and death
trapped in a frame; his goal, exact ornithology
but something, too, of the bird's own character
amply infused with the artist's undying verve.

**3**

Ironic, yes: Audubon killed the birds he loved
to bring them to life in his art — shot,
skewered, wired on a position board, vivid
until the colors drained out. He had twelve hours
or less to set their eternal likenesses down.
The great white heron's multiple whites converge
in a uniform shade with a few dirty feathers.
His saffron, vise-tight beak and pink tongue
clamp a rose-yellow fish, whose marbly eye
is a tiny version of the stalking fisher's.
Any resemblance eludes the predator,
whose triumph dwarfs a pea-green bay in the Keys.
Soon the heron will lift on outstretched wings.
Only a random age-stain sears this page.

**4**

At last, a peaceful scene! Four spotted grouse
are reveling together in the underbrush
of bushes and serpentine vines; their camouflage
suggests they've found a protected resting place.
The scarlet berries of the moonseed plant
drop like pendants before their luck-struck eyes,
welcome assurance they can relax and feast
for hours there. Audubon described them
as gallinaceous birds, like pheasant or quail.
He painted them unassuming, edibly plump.
His care with the curve of tail, tincture of beak,
the attention to throat, scapular, and claw
instruct us about a salient feature of love:
how its looks reside in the smallest detail.

## 5

Am I guilty of killing Audubon's art
that tracked elusive birds, some now extinct,
by pinning down his prints into my poem?
If so, my trespass springs from a human need
to say what quickens the mind and heart
or thrills the eye: beauty should be recorded;
ponder its source and how it was achieved —
unforeseen, improbable, phoenix-like.
Though Audubon died wealthy, his art affirmed
by worldly success, he dreamed his large-scale work
*The Birds of America* at his lowest point, at his nadir,
in midlife and bankrupt, confined in debtors' jail,
where saving imagination summoned his will
and from a window ledge in his cell took flight.

*For Aileen Ward*

## Night Birding, Trinidad

Under Moriche palms where macaws flew in
to roost and the Southern Cross emerged,
we stood in a patch of scrub savannah,
while our guide called for the screech owl

with a tape-recorded "who" —
*who-who-who-who* — like the start of the sixties song
"Wipe Out." No one moved.
We stood in darkness, each with different thoughts,

far from home, each with different forgotten
concerns, our only job to remain still
and wait. The owl moved in, close, a whirring uprush,
but disclosed nothing more,

then moved off. So we moved,
forming the same horseshoe up the road.
Again, a near brush, a felt proximity,
but not the revelation. What did we want

to find? The owl outside
or, like Wordsworth, something inside,
long flown? Or maybe nothing known before,
just the hoped-for, yet-to-come.

## The Scan

We were given these instruments after your birth:
syringe, Tegaderm, heparin flush.
This morning, I found them behind the file cabinet.
Dare I throw them out?
I am a superstitious girl.

When I stood in the parted door and gave you up
for the scan, anesthetized, dye-injected,
your one-year-old body sang
its sweet, green galaxy of bone.
In the corridor, children sat tethered to IVs,

one in a party dress, incongruous as her lack of hair.
Slumped in your room's black corner,
I thought: nothing can save us
unbelievers. I am not like Abraham.

Yet a voice entreated:
*Come with me — just this far.*
I went to the cool, metal table,
where you lay in the dark.
*Haven't I always taken care of her?*

*Isn't she still here?*
When I looked,
I had to say yes,
even as the clicking machine
aimed at your chest.

## The News

She was going about an ordinary day,
pondering dinner, washing a dish,
or sweeping the floor. Maybe
she was standing in the garden
or had come in from the garden
to sit by the window and rest.
Perhaps she had taken up a book
or remembered the unfinished sewing
when she encountered an angel
in the middle of the room.

Of course, she was shocked,
though the angel offered a host
of assurances. Whatever she thought,
she didn't hang her head in chagrin,
collapse in a rattled heap,
or race from the house. Neither
did she act like she'd won the lottery
and could lord it over everyone,

but, no doubt, picked up the sewing,
the book, the broom, or the dish
in which she glimpsed her reflection,
a woman without any special features
except for the yellow nimbus now
hovering around her head, someone
who didn't even try to strike
a deal with the messenger,
though she was certainly going to
give up a lot being part of this plan.

## The Harvesters

In Bruegel's *The Harvesters*, two birds break
out of the wheat. Disturbed into the hot,
clear air, a portion of time, they turn
in the direction of roads laid out
like wishbones beyond the neighboring farms,
church, and one heavily-laden wagon
practically home. The roads wind toward
an indented harbor, scattered with boats
lying at anchor or pulling up anchor
under the cloudless, late-summer sky.
The half-harvested field stands
like a topiary, like the noon meal
en route to extinction, anxiously taken
under a crooked tree, where vertical wheat

stacks are as tall as the people.
Piles of horizontal sheaves need binding.
The amber remnant of ground cut in quadrants
unfolds like a mapped country. Into the foreground
where most of the harvesters sit,
cross-legged and aproned, their sickles
thrown down, a stoop-shouldered, middle-aged
man lugs water. How easy it is to see
the harvesters' fatigue. One in particular,
dead-center, sprawls in the shade,
eyes shut, too tired to eat; he fits
like a jigsaw piece completing the big
picture, where all falls simply into
what has been done and whatever remains.

## Activity That Defies Loss

It is good some nights
to sit in the lamplight
reading the dictionary,

because it reminds me
(having just had to look up
the meaning of "hasp")

how impoverished my life
is without the words
I don't know to define it —

words I have never read,
alas, much less used,
or have seen, but felt

too lazy to go find,
or if not too slothlike,
have now forgotten,

since I never employed them
gainfully. Most people
would not understand

the thrill of finding
"harrow" and considering
under what circumstances

it might become "harrowing,"
or beholding "hogfish,"
wondering if this second

it might be gliding
over a Caribbean reef.
I can dawdle between

"holotype" and "holy ghost,"
"herdic" and "hypogeal"
for hours, then slip to

"limacine" and "limbate,"
dreaming of what I've missed,
knowing that tomorrow

I can easily return
to retrieve it,
possibly stumbling on

a half familiar phrase
like "ionic bond,"
whose mere pronunciation

recalls eighth-grade
chemistry. There I am,
staring out the window,

imagining a time, maybe
this one, when I can
do exactly what I want.

## Cleo

Three identical stripes ring
my tabby's forelegs; symmetrical spots
sit on each side of her nose,
from which glide elegant whiskers.
Their bearing reveals inner weather:
horizontal for contentment,
drooping for a mood out-of-sorts.
Love's contortionist, she will fold
herself like a cockle shell
to fit beside me where I read,
and I must take quiet satisfaction
in this affectionate display,
since wanting more would invite
a swat or snap, then make her flee.
Her eyes, creased in tiny boomerangs,
open to say, this is perfect,
resting side by side, acknowledging
need, but not going overboard.

Now, she stares as if I were the pet
and she expected some trick.
Obligingly, I pull the gummy label
from my book, wad it up, one end still stuck
to the cover. She extends her paw
like a croupier's stick, but failing
to remove it, licks her fur
as if that's what she intended.
Her steel-wool tongue smoothes the paw
which yesterday plucked a hamster
from its cage when my daughter wasn't looking
and dropped it at my feet.
The death-paw cannot undo the label,
my gift to her. She grooms herself again
for effect, regards me coolly,
then drifts to sleep like a fat putto
as though promising later to explain
the deep mysteries of our commerce.

## The Leap

The sign next to the springboard faith reads:
*Jump right in*. I'd rather it said *No swimming
without a lifeguard on duty*. This matters
only because it relates to the fear of death

which nobody really ever discusses. At parties,
we never follow a handshake with "I'm scared
of dying, aren't you?" On good days, I can overlook
the question; on bad ones, it rises with vengeance,

always at 32,000 feet. I never assume the jarring
movement of the plane is normal, like hitting
a speed bump too quickly in a car. I'm sure
we're seconds away from a nose dive. I start praying

and bargaining for another chance, one close call
for a cast-off vice. Why can't I make peace
with a fate everyone meets, consider it no more
than sleep? Why couldn't I have learned the secret

from a relative or friend who's gone before?
Maybe I'll arrive at such affliction, that ceasing
to exist will seem like a serious improvement,
like my great-aunt who averred, before passing away,

"I've had enough," or my grandmother who asked,
"Are you homesick?" I tried comforting her
by saying, "We *are* home," though I suspect she was
pondering another address, being almost there.

Expressing the fear is a kind of release,
a first step, but not full solace. Putting aside
the assuaging petition, an agreeable hope,
speculation, even the witness of saints,

I will not be at ease until I face my end
with equanimity, feel a good regard for that place —
if it is a place where we can never be quite
certain we'll see each other again.

In the meantime, I'll sit in my lawn chair,
pace the grounds, even approach the ladder to count
the rungs. The signs of the faithful abound,
though I am terrified of heights and full of doubt.

## Sign

The foreign artist, racked by Tourette's,
repeated loud, monotonous activities
like climbing stairs. He would scream
in the room whenever we gathered
to talk. Most of us, including myself,
said he had no right to disturb us.
We tried to avoid his erratic behavior,
given our need for safety in the presence
of what we did not understand.
Yet when, near the end of his stay,
he displayed his paintings of buildings
whose many doors were shut, only
a single window open on the highest floor,
I knew he was really an angel,

like the very old man with enormous wings
in the García Márquez story,
who fell face down in the mud
one night, unable to rise, impeded
by his filthy, half-plucked feathers.
How the townspeople gossiped.
They tried to put names to the creature
which didn't speak Latin as an angel should,
perform the predictable miracles,
or offer the meanest reward,
except to the owner of the yard
who charged admission to see
the castaway locked in a chicken coop,
eating his eggplant mush.

What crossed the mind of the yard owner's wife
as her unsightly burden lumbered
into the air until he was a dot on the horizon,
García Márquez doesn't say. What any of us
thought watching our annoyance leave
in the taxi's dust, no one will know,
but the young man never made us feel guilty.
He extended a pardon we didn't deserve,
giving each of us his business card
*

and an offer to visit his home in Singapore.
I doubt I'll get to his native land,
though I'm keeping his card as a sign
of the distance I still have to travel
between here and the bright city Compassion.

## Flash

Beyond the screen a yellow finch, spurred
by the sun after a long winter, flitted
from the bare kousa to the feeder, replete
with thistle. She was feeding and building
her nest with such fervor, it staggered me,
for I am a timorous human, able to imagine
all the difficult routes to ruin. Curse the restive
mind, memory, fear. How improved I'd be
going on just instinct, season-tuned, not
second guessing, hoping for the crime not to be
committed, the injury done, or sweet life taken
by accident and time — like the hyacinths
which keep extending themselves because
it is April, despite the forecast of snow.

## Amulet Market

I might have purchased a charm against
any malady or threat. How sorry I am
I didn't read Thai, for if I had, right now
I'd own amulets against headaches and plane crashes.
If I'd known the future, I'd have bought one
against panic for my daughter, stomach pain
for a friend, anxiety about money for my beloved.
All I acquired, a thimble-size Buddha, I plucked
in haste from a straw basket. Who knows
what he guards me from — my greedy self?
He recalls the monks with only three possessions:
sandals, robe, bowl, and the greatest good —
peace, the way one of them lay down easily
in the middle of the crowded market to sleep.

## The Alleluia Man

Despite my inch-thick windows
muffling traffic, tonight
the cry of our local lunatic

seeps through: "Alleluia!
Alleluia!" making me wonder
what failures swamped him:

pink slip, ruined marriage,
childhood abuse — some rare
combination of losses?

Or maybe a blessing transpired
and like Saint Francis preaching
to birds, his head a flame

of ecstasy, he has spoken
with God. By all accounts,
it takes just once — the rest

is easy: sell what you have;
hoist the cross; pack nothing
for your trip. Each day he stands

by the subway station, dressed
in his suit and tie, holding
the Bible and a shopping bag.

He looks ineffectual
in the fast tide of commuters,
not the type to command birds

to the earth's four corners,
convert Wall Street sultans
or alter a robber's heart,

not to mention receive the stigmata —
his proof of a higher world.
On the other hand, he's managed

to shout his way into my life
so that hearing him, I open
the window if only to check

what he's wearing. How many souls
will he collect, calling "God loves you"?
Crank or prophet, he's making

a start in the same brown suit,
his book raised toward Heaven, and rain
falling on his fiery praise.

## Last Entry

> ... *the whole width of the world has passed behind us —*
> *except this broad ocean.*
> — Amelia Earhart

Only the living want answers.
You, figuring what happened,
will arrive at conjecture,
some plausible account
that allows you to quell
the insistent question.

I can tell you this —
my time was my time,
unwasted by worry or regret.
I was never bored.

Of course you are mobilizing
an expensive search;
books will interpret events.
Years hence there may be a way
to raise my plane from the ocean floor.

You will find it oddly still
intact, a monument to the deep,
rooted in sea fans,
circled by moon-eyed fish.

I will not be here
though you may retrieve my log.
Shall I say we exhausted our fuel,
the sunrise stunned me,
Noonan misjudged?
I was tired of the punishing route,

the equator's heat, nausea,
tired, too, of my husband
pushing for air records and money.
Let's say when events conspired,

I embraced them.
As for the actual moment,
the only one there is,
the one you really came to learn about,
nothing I can say will touch it.

## III. War Remnants

## Two Halves

Half of me bore a suspicion
the other half denied, trying
to loosen it like a knot in a chain,

a suspicion as black as the tarmac
my father crossed to his fighter jet.
The world would be impossible

without him, half of me thought,
but the inkling, once sprouted, started
to spread like bamboo, cluttering

and choking the grassy bank
until it becomes landscape, a fact.
Why think of this now?

half of me asks, craving knowledge.
The other half draws a blank.

## Stopping at the True, the Good, the Beautiful Company in Bac Ninh

After a cruise on the *Halong Dream*,
the guide informs us we will stop
at a typical silk and embroidery store,
only not exactly typical, since

its employees are orphans and children,
maimed by war after their mothers, exposed
to Agent Orange, bore them. Here,
they live and work, relatively secure.

Young and not-so-young are bent
over whirring machines and finished cloth
that they slowly embellish by hand.
I veer into the finished-products aisle —

dressing gowns, *ao dai*, table linens —
searching for something inexpensive,
lightweight, and easy to pack,
like finger towels, which a British lady

says she had hoped to find because
they make the perfect house gift.
I agree. The manager following us
has no frame of reference, suggesting

a laundry bag — three different sizes.
I choose a little one with drawstrings,
imagining what I could put inside —
some potpourri, bangles, tea?

Or perhaps regret, longing, and guilt.
I buy a dozen, each with a scene
of Vietnam, carefully stitched
in thread so fine the eyes could dim

putting it there: a woman wearing
her conical hat, with her buffalo,
in a field of rice, which my father saw
and knew, high and small, from the air.

## My Father Meets Amelia Earhart

After my father's plane crashed in the Pacific,
I used to think how sad that he was
alone when he died, strapped
in his fighter jet, latitude and longitude
unknown, his recovery barred,

no one to bear his casket to the family plot.
Yet now I imagine Amelia with Noonan
in tow, on hand to greet him.
After twenty-nine years in a similar fix,
she welcomed a traveler who shared her passion.

He would have liked her, of course,
and she him, both being thirty-nine, handsome,
death-wed too early, like Icarus.
They could talk shop — his Skyhawk
versus her Electra, compare hops and their DFCs,

play rummy. In time, they would grow
philosophical over how events played out,
how a lack of choice brought them there
(tragedy's common element) or so they thought —
she with her compulsion to follow through

despite the signs of a doomed endeavor
and he with his outsize sense of duty
to lead his squadron back to the Tonkin Gulf.
His father, the admiral with Pentagon ties,
could have pulled strings, and G.P. counseled

Amelia in Lae to stop. But no,
locked into circumstances, they cradled
their fates. And still, they look on the bright side:
neither suffered the indignities of old age;
both became legends in people's minds.

He would have been pleased to idle
with this pioneer of aviation who chirped
"Violet" and "Cheerio" on take-off,
the first woman to lecture the middies at Annapolis.
If he sent me a postcard, it might say:

*Your grandfather may have posed
for a photograph with Will Rogers
on the flight deck,
but I'm spending eternity
with the Queen of the Air.*

## Water Buffalo

He lies cooling in mud, his head just visible.
My father bought his carved likeness years ago.
Chihuahua size, he stood on our living-room chest,
massive horns swept up in a lethal headdress,
or so I thought, his eyes large and sad. I want
my picture taken, so I squat by the water,

nervously smiling, asking my husband to hurry,
click the shutter. Before he can, the buffalo
stirs to climb the bank, which I hear and leap back,
making the Vietnamese gathered around laugh:
*He won't hurt you. He only wants to smell your skin
which is new to him.* Poor buffalo, gentle,

misunderstood, my alarm sends him reeling.
I extend my arm and hold myself rock still
as he rumbles out once more, all grey one ton,
snorting and breathing me in without censure
or grudge, his breath an unexpected answer to
my ignorance, his hide tough velvet like forgiveness.

## At the War Remnants Museum, Saigon

I will not look at the bomb
used for attacking motor vehicles or trains,
how it cuts animals and persons
with six razors opening
like a turning helicopter blade.

I will not look at the large striated explosives,
or the small, smooth orange one
that resembles a football,
with its muzzle velocity
of 1200 meters per second.

I will not stand long
in front of the napalm victims
with their hands wrapped like cocoons,
bodies marred beyond reconstruction,
the baby whose skin is gone.

I will not gaze at the XM41E2
gravel mine, dropped by AD-6 planes
over roads, populous towns,
and densely wooded areas,
the mines buried still in the land.

Ruined villages, temples, homes —
I will certainly not look at
the children touched by Agent Orange,
the malformed head floating
in an airtight jar. I will not look

at the rocket launcher,
containers of chemicals being prepared
for Operation Ranch Hand
out of Da Nang, all toxins
while US and ARVN soldiers wear masks.

## III. WAR REMNANTS

Defoliants, little dress burned,
a child's sandal, a woman's face
with a gun to her head at the Massacre of Huong Dien,
the girl imploring troops,
*Don't kill my father.*

Do not tarry here in history's dark rooms
when all that is behind us
and the sun is bursting outside
where Hung, our driver, who says he was
a VC guerrilla, smokes in the shade.

## Little Exchange

At Hai Van Pass,
U.S. bunkers
guarded Da Nang,
while VC slept
beneath by day,
and, in the hills
adjacent, snaked
the Ho Chi Minh trail.
Nothing remains
of our presence there —
today's rest stop,
tomorrow's condo.
Souvenir tables
with key chains,
tiger balm,
Buddhas and pearls
line the walk
to the restroom,
where a lady
about my age
asks a question.
"You Vietnamese?
Your skin like mine,"
she says, "your hair
black, not blonde."
"No," I answer,
"I am American."
She wants my money.
"Look, many gifts."
"Later," I lie.
Who can blame her,
or me, who leaves
empty-handed?
"Do not forget me,"
she calls,
"I not forget you."

## The Moving Wall

Today in Malta, New York,
hundreds of people file
past the half-size replica

of the Vietnam Memorial.
Tomorrow, it moves to New Jersey,
where, having been broken

down into manageable parts,
it will be reassembled —
a moving wall of names,

58,159 the paper says
and too many tears
to account for. With this,

we recognize the dead,
who did nothing wrong
but assent to duty;

all the commissioned
and drafted died so others,
head-down in books

or richly deferred, could turn
from the screaming head-
lines of the day, which lied.

Pricked into conscience too late
and missing the mark,
we hailed a Hollywood actress

who chained herself to the USS *Enterprise*
as if war were a stage set,
and troops in the Tonkin Gulf

preferred their fate to hers,
built on prerogative, like us stateside,
hating ourselves, blaming

the soldiers so much that
when they came home,
they knew enough to exchange their uniforms

for civilian clothes in airport restrooms.
Thus we handle our shame —
find the scapegoats, then

build a wall to honor them.
Make it move like a shade
bringing relief from the sun;

let it fold its wings like a moth
passing from room to room,
sparing us long-term grief

or the need to live with
a mistake so large, should we
acknowledge it or bend

on collective knees to ask
forgiveness would render the wall,
however moving, obsolete.

*Saratoga Springs*
*June 12, 2006*

## Eye Exam

How easy it was to venerate my father,
because he put his life on the line.
Sent to war, he went and died, leaving us
his cruise box, air medals, legacy:
a heartthrob uniformed hero lost too soon.

Yet how should I view my mother, left
to piece back the bits, entomb her grief,
and guide her children's riddled passage
to adulthood, then her job done, sit
shell-shocked in the deafening absence?

The technician adjusts the trial glasses
and tells me to look at the chart,
a blur of script I can just make out
if I squint. "Do you see more clearly?"
she asks. "No? What about now?"

**IV. Love Work**

## First Kiss

When Raymond glided by me across the playing field, I chased him
    like a jet off radar
to plant the ultimate sting on his cheek: a kiss that burned him
    to a blossom of tears.
"What drove you to that?" the teacher inquired, pulling us both aside,
    his small shoulders heaving,
my eyes scanning the air for a reason. It sprang from the boys'
    chanting, "Girls have cooties."
If I had them, why shouldn't he? After school, Mother's withering
    look met me at the door.
She forced me to confess the recess affair to my father,
    the squadron commander,
God's right-hand man, my prank now promoted to a top-ranking sin.
    Love and sex dove under-
ground, buried deep as my spinster great-aunts, though I recall once
    during my college years,
when I came home too late, Mother asked if she should screw a scarlet
    bulb in the front-yard lamp —
Did I plan to turn our street into a red-light district?
    Raymond, wherever you are, whatever your last name is,
you are the pyre on which I throw each guilt-ridden kiss.

## Desire

Because I longed for the vista of neighboring fields
and roads, the Severn River beyond, I climbed
our apple tree, its blossoms a velvet snow
falling out of season. The bees drummed low,
Look here! Each sallied forth, fat as a grape.
I reached for one the way I cupped the keyhole to glimpse
my father after his bath. He sensed I was there
and opened the door with harsh scolding. Off-balance,
summit-near, I plunged through the sharp branches,
landing on a stick that cut my eye. Butterfly-bandaged
after emergency care, I dozed in my curtained room,
caught in a half-dream of starry flowers and bees.
The wished-for view that could have claimed my sight
left instead one barely perceptible scar.

## Weatherworn

The air was closer than a terrarium's
where bits of transplanted green moss thrive
causing beads of moisture to grow like tears
upon the glass, then slowly descend the sides —
a small tide, unable to stop or wipe away.
The sky cohered in a charcoal canopy
oppressing the flinty stands of paralyzed fir
and song-spent birds. The fountain's naiad looked
tired of balancing the loaded atmosphere
on two slim marble hands — a noble gesture.
Over the world's back a wheel of thunder groaned.
Whether I paced my breathless room or parched lawn
driven by heat, longing for rain,
I held your body's fierce proximity at bay.

## In Mountain Air

The field slopes to a river
camouflaged by summer birch and jack pine,

darkly braided except where light breaks
touching the smooth rocks, the bracken.

Through mown hay, a man and woman walk,
carrying part of their lives.

The only sounds are the trees stirring
and grasshoppers reaching new ground.

Their footsteps do not fracture
any of the mountain's certain stillness;

the grass springs up, covering their path
as the roadside inn fades behind.

This time, when they reach the river,
she does not turn away, though she intended

merely to say, *how lovely the evening,
how level the light traversing the field.*

*My life is fixed as a table setting,
the distance from the house to the barn.*

## Seaweed Weather

**1**

For three days we've been enveloped by rain
thrashing the house, flattening the sand dunes.
Battleship waves are crashing in tiers of porcelain,
dove-white foam that turns dirty-brown as it's strewn
over mountains of seaweed. Should we regret
the scant shore left? The current could swallow us whole.
The wind's exhale in the volleyball net
strains its fastenings and shakes the two poles.
Somewhere, halyards telegraph a high-pitched —
paean or jeremiad? As ligustrum knocks
the pane, an owl, rarely heard in these parts,
repeats there is nothing but trouble docked
here, alongside a wish, hunkering down
in seaweed weather, to ride the dark squall out.

**2**

At morning an unforeseen clearing of sky
entices us to drag the folding chairs,
umbrella, raft, and towels down to the beach.
I station myself at the tidal edge, reading
a forgettable book while you claim higher ground —
*Madame Bovary* (in French). Who will ask
the other, first, to swim? Once heat and time conspire
we're wading through the lukewarm slough
past argument and thought, diving into
huge Atlantic rollers, the *pièce de résistance*:
a sandbar rising, saving us from an undertow
and depths of the other which lead to exhaustion.
For hours we had desired this common ground,
though we could not be certain it would find us.

**3**

Returning to the house, we can measure
the toll of the northeaster that might have become
a full-blown hurricane: the dunes are carved
into a parenthesis where the waves went in,
carrying the sand south to another beach.
Our neighbor's catamaran has tipped on its side.
Kelp and sargassum ride the deep shell-bed
with broken conchs and collectible sharks' teeth.
"It could have been worse" is what survivors say
and point to what is left: the sea oats holding
their own, an endangered flora illegal to pick,
its slender filament belied by the root
keeping it there, stopping permanent erosion,
and, of course, the weathered gray bulkhead steps.

**4**

At night, after a dinner of shrimp and wine,
we comb the shore whose tides have taken the seaweed.
Proverbial stars emerge the way they do
in a planetarium — on cue, extreme in numbers
and light, suggesting a message that we might read
if schooled in the names of constellations.
In spite of ignorance we survive, in spite of
our limitations; the stars do not begrudge us,
neither the moon that rises out of the sea,
or seems to, turning the surface phosphorous.
I'd rather be lucky than right, my father said,
and I am lucky with you; arm in arm,
we hurry to bed where the palms outside our window
wrestle with a light wind, and the stars shine in.

## Story of Us

Would we have stepped into the little boat
of marriage then knowing what we do now —
how narrow the watchband gunwales, precarious
the balance, one of us in the bow, the other
at the stern, changing places with difficulty,
always swaying, headed for rock-strewn rapids
or battling currents, blistering our hands,
afraid mortal falls might appear at the bend?

We would never have felt the sweet night lulls
blanketed with stars, found the moon rising
settling our angers, our grief, witnessed
the landscape alter along banks we skirted
and touched. If we'd stayed on the dock, untraveled,
unspent, we'd have no beginning, expect no end.

## Lesson

Everyone's enrolled in the school of loss,
the instruments of study, heart and mind,
applied to life experience. Me? I've been
a student a long time; I'm taking too long
to graduate. How cross my accomplished principal
has grown, weary of making me write
"Nothing gold can stay" as many times as it takes.
Pages accrue on my desk in the waning sun.
When she dismisses me, my cramped hand aches.
I almost believe repetition has driven
the lesson home, till outside under the stars
and the moon's two profiled faces locked
in a white, new kiss, a reasonable mind is
helpless to tamp the heart's rich howl.

## Plaza View

Last night a crowd assembled here
behind a lank ghost on stilts
whose arms of worn-out bed sheets
billowed in the cold air.
Heralding a new year,
it sailed around the fountain,
down the darkened avenue
where curved street lamps stood
like question marks.
Skaters on the frozen pond
stopped their continuous circles
for the fireworks blossoming
north of them and shortly
dissolving on the sky.
Beneath that panoply we watched
the horse-drawn carriages until
each grew too small, the hour
too late. Something about one carriage
stopped at the curb, its dappled
gray horse with head bent to feed,
something about the driver
having a long smoke,
his face turned moonward
made us know nothing
we could see had changed,
not inside where we turned our quilted
bedcover back, nor out
where ice skaters skated in time
to the distant, inaudible music.

## Love Work

My love, travel to me quickly for time
strikes like a ruler slapped on a pupil's hand.
Put work aside, worry, too, all the Midwest
Presbyterian principles I once loved you for
and still do. I have learned there's more
to our being here, so tenuous and brief,
than securing sums for retirement. After that, we'll be
past caring about all we own save each other,
hand to hand, and what we may have stored
from the grind, grit, from gratifying sweet
instances, compounded through desire and will.
Tick tick goes the time clock. I hear it
in the recent statements of our industry
collected fast in a binder like a rebuke.

# Biographical Note

Gardner McFall is the author of *The Pilot's Daughter* (Time Being Books). She is also the editor of *Made with Words*, a prose miscellany, by May Swenson (University of Michigan Press), the author of two children's books, *Jonathan's Cloud* (Harper & Row) and *Naming the Animals* (Viking), and the librettist for *Amelia*, an opera commissioned by Seattle Opera, with music by Daron Hagen. Ms. McFall, who has received a "Discovery"/ The Nation award and the *Missouri Review*'s Thomas McAfee Prize for Poetry, earned her master's degree from the Writing Seminars at The Johns Hopkins University and her doctorate, in English, from New York University. She lives in New York City and teaches at Hunter College.

# Other Poetry and Short Fictions Available from Time Being Books

**Yakov Azriel**
In the Shadow of a Burning Bush: Poems on Exodus
Threads from a Coat of Many Colors: Poems on Genesis

**Edward Boccia**
No Matter How Good the Light Is: Poems by a Painter

**Louis Daniel Brodsky**
The Capital Café: Poems of Redneck, U.S.A.
Catchin' the Drift o' the Draft *(short fictions)*
Combing Florida's Shores: Poems of Two Lifetimes
The Complete Poems of Louis Daniel Brodsky: Volumes One–Four
Dine-Rite: Breakfast Poems
Disappearing in Mississippi Latitudes: Volume Two of *A Mississippi Trilogy*
The Eleventh Lost Tribe: Poems of the Holocaust
Falling from Heaven: Holocaust Poems of a Jew and a Gentile *(Brodsky and Heyen)*
Forever, for Now: Poems for a Later Love
Four and Twenty Blackbirds Soaring
Gestapo Crows: Holocaust Poems
A Gleam in the Eye: Poems for a First Baby
Leaky Tubs *(short fictions)*
Mississippi Vistas: Volume One of *A Mississippi Trilogy*
Mistress Mississippi: Volume Three of *A Mississippi Trilogy*
Nuts to You! *(short fictions)*
Once upon a Small-Town Time: Poems of America's Heartland
Paper-Whites for Lady Jane: Poems of a Midlife Love Affair
Peddler on the Road: Days in the Life of Willy Sypher
Pigskinizations *(short fictions)*
Rated Xmas *(short fictions)*
Shadow War: A Poetic Chronicle of September 11 and Beyond, Volumes One–Five
Showdown with a Cactus: Poems Chronicling the Prickly Struggle Between the Forces of Dubya-ness and Enlightenment, 2003–2006
Still Wandering in the Wilderness: Poems of the Jewish Diaspora
This Here's a Merica *(short fictions)*
The Thorough Earth
Three Early Books of Poems by Louis Daniel Brodsky, 1967–1969: *The Easy Philosopher*, *"A Hard Coming of It" and Other Poems*, and *The Foul Rag-and-Bone Shop*
Toward the Torah, Soaring: Poems of the Renascence of Faith
A Transcendental Almanac: Poems of Nature
Voice Within the Void: Poems of *Homo supinus*

# 866-840-4334
# http://www.timebeing.com

**Louis Daniel Brodsky** *(continued)*
The World Waiting to Be: Poems About the Creative Process
Yellow Bricks *(short fictions)*
You Can't Go Back, Exactly

**Harry James Cargas** *(editor)*
Telling the Tale: A Tribute to Elie Wiesel on the Occasion of His 65th Birthday — Essays, Reflections, and Poems

**Judith Chalmer**
Out of History's Junk Jar: Poems of a Mixed Inheritance

**Gerald Early**
How the War in the Streets Is Won: Poems on the Quest of Love and Faith

**Gary Fincke**
Blood Ties: Working-Class Poems

**Charles Adés Fishman**
Blood to Remember: American Poets on the Holocaust *(editor)*
Chopin's Piano

**CB Follett**
Hold and Release

**Albert Goldbarth**
A Lineage of Ragpickers, Songpluckers, Elegiasts & Jewelers: Selected Poems of Jewish Family Life, 1973–1995

**Robert Hamblin**
From the Ground Up: Poems of One Southerner's Passage to Adulthood
Keeping Score: Sports Poems for Every Season

**William Heyen**
Erika: Poems of the Holocaust
Falling from Heaven: Holocaust Poems of a Jew and a Gentile *(Brodsky and Heyen)*
The Host: Selected Poems, 1965–1990
Pterodactyl Rose: Poems of Ecology
Ribbons: The Gulf War — A Poem

866-840-4334
http://www.timebeing.com

**Ted Hirschfield**
German Requiem: Poems of the War and the Atonement of a Third Reich Child

**Virginia V. James Hlavsa**
Waking October Leaves: Reanimations by a Small-Town Girl

**Rodger Kamenetz**
The Missing Jew: New and Selected Poems
Stuck: Poems Midlife

**Norbert Krapf**
Blue-Eyed Grass: Poems of Germany
Looking for God's Country
Somewhere in Southern Indiana: Poems of Midwestern Origins

**Adrian C. Louis**
Blood Thirsty Savages

**Leo Luke Marcello**
Nothing Grows in One Place Forever: Poems of a Sicilian American

**Gardner McFall**
The Pilot's Daughter

**Joseph Meredith**
Hunter's Moon: Poems from Boyhood to Manhood

**Ben Milder**
The Good Book Also Says . . . : Numerous Humorous Poems Inspired by the New Testament
The Good Book Says . . . : Light Verse to Illuminate the Old Testament
Love Is Funny, Love Is Sad
What's So Funny About the Golden Years
The Zoo You Never Gnu: A Mad Menagerie of Bizarre Beasts and Birds

**Charles Muñoz**
Fragments of a Myth: Modern Poems on Ancient Themes

**866-840-4334**
**http://www.timebeing.com**

**Micheal O'Siadhail**
The Gossamer Wall: Poems in Witness to the Holocaust

**Joseph Stanton**
A Field Guide to the Wildlife of Suburban Oʻahu
Imaginary Museum: Poems on Art

**Susan Terris**
Contrariwise